To Danny:

Books can
take you to many
places, people, and
things.

Read, read, read

Love,
Mrs Vikis 1970!

Answers About
BIRDS and
ANIMALS

Written by ROBERT MATHEWSON
and MARTIN L. KEEN

Illustrated by WALTER FERGUSON
and NED SMITH

GROSSET & DUNLAP
NEW YORK
A National General Company

Library of Congress Catalog Card Number: 78-122564

CONTENTS

RHAMPHORHYNCHUS

PTERANODON

ORNITHOLESTES

WHICH CAME FIRST—THE BIRD OR THE EGG?

It all started about 200 million years ago when the dinosaurs, which were reptiles, roamed the earth. At this time, some of the smaller dinosaurs made their homes among the rocks in high cliffs. This kind of habitat offered protection from the large meat-eating dinosaurs that were too heavy to climb across the loose rocks.

It was here that the *Pterodactyls* (ter-o-DACK-tils) were found. They were flying reptiles, and flight helped them to escape an enemy or to swoop down and catch food. Some of the *Pterodactyls* (which means "wing finger") grew to enormous size. *Ornithostoma* (or-nee-THOS-to-ma) was the largest of all flying creatures. The present-day albatross, with its wingspread of approximately eleven feet, is small compared to *Ornithostoma* (which means "bird mouth"). *Ornithostoma* was born with a ten-foot wingspread and, as an adult, had a wingspread of over twenty feet.

ARCHAEOPTERYX

ARCHAEOPTERYX

ICHTHYORNIS

HESPERORNIS

During this period, many small reptiles were developing a character which was eventually to separate them from the reptile group. They were slowly evolving feathers. *Archaeopteryx* (ar-kee-OP-ter-iks, meaning "ancient wing") was the most familiar of these early birdlike reptiles. It had large and perfectly formed feathers on its wings and tail and had also developed birdlike legs. Other kinds, such as *Odontotormae* (O-DON-toe-tor-may, meaning "toothed bird") and *Ichthyornis* (ik-thee-OR-nis, meaning "fish bird"), had even more birdlike characteristics and were about the size of present-day gulls.

All of the early reptiles had one trait in common—they laid eggs. The next time you hear the question, "Which came first—the bird or the egg?" you will know the answer:

The reptile came first.

WHAT GOOD ARE BIRDS?

Today there are about nine thousand different species of birds in all sizes, forms and colors. There are gaudily colored parrots and macaws in tropical America; large flightless cassowaries and emus in Australia; tiny warblers and sparrows in temperate America; soaring gulls and vultures throughout the world; and plump chickens and turkeys in the farmyard.

Let us suppose that there had never been turkeys anywhere on earth. We would not miss them. If there were no woodpeckers or other insect-eating birds, though, it wouldn't be long before the whole world would be overrun by many hundreds of thousands of troublesome insects, eating away at plants and trees.

Anyone who has heard the *rat-a-tat-tat* of the woodpecker has had the opportunity to see at first hand the great insect-eating value of birds. A strong beak and neck muscles are the tools of the woodpecker. They enable the bird to cut its way through the tree bark to the insect feeding on the wood below. A special tongue, which is barbed, helps the woodpecker to stab, withdraw, and eat the insect. Most birds, at some time in their lives, feed upon insects.

Birds also act as scavengers. Species such as gulls, vultures, crows, as well as hawks and owls, help to keep our woodlands and fields free of carrion (the flesh of dead animals).

Other important things about birds, particularly to those who spend some time watching them, are their bright, cheery colors and habits, and their beautiful songs.

There are about 375 species of woodpeckers. Their sharp bills bore into the bark of trees for insects. Below are some insect pests eaten by birds.

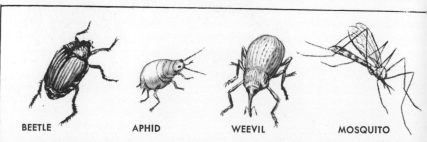

BEETLE   APHID   WEEVIL   MOSQUITO

WHY SHOULD BIRDS BE WATCHED AND STUDIED?

Watching birds, learning to identify the different kinds by their shape, color and song, is a hobby which can bring many moments of real pleasure. It can change an ordinary walk through the park, the woodland, or even the city street, into an exciting adventure. The ways of these feathered fliers are soon learned and some become old "friends." Whether they hop, run or walk, and whether they fly in spurts or straight lines, are some of the habits which aid in identifying each kind.

Even their songs will become familiar. The music of the wood thrush is pleasant to all. The song soon becomes associated with the bird and is often used in helping to identify it. In the park, the robins and sparrows will be known; in the woodland, the thrush and towhee; in the field, the meadowlark and pheasant; and at the beach, the gull and pelican.

Birds are with us winter, spring, summer and fall, and every nook and corner of our earth has its bird population. The only requirement for seeing them is to do it quietly. A few moments spent standing, sitting, or slowly walking in a park, an open field or woodland grove will reveal many more birds than will hours of strenuous hiking. Birds have keen eyesight and hearing and are very timid animals. They will avoid a noisy observer.

A good bird watcher studies birds in his area. Repeated trips along the same paths and trails disclose where and upon what they feed, where they bathe and drink, where they nest, and even in what trees they choose to sing. This kind of observing will be rewarded by the discovery of many facts about their habits. Not all of the breeding, nesting and feeding habits of birds are known, and good observers can add much to the store of scientific knowledge.

WHERE DO BIRDS BEGIN THEIR LIVES?

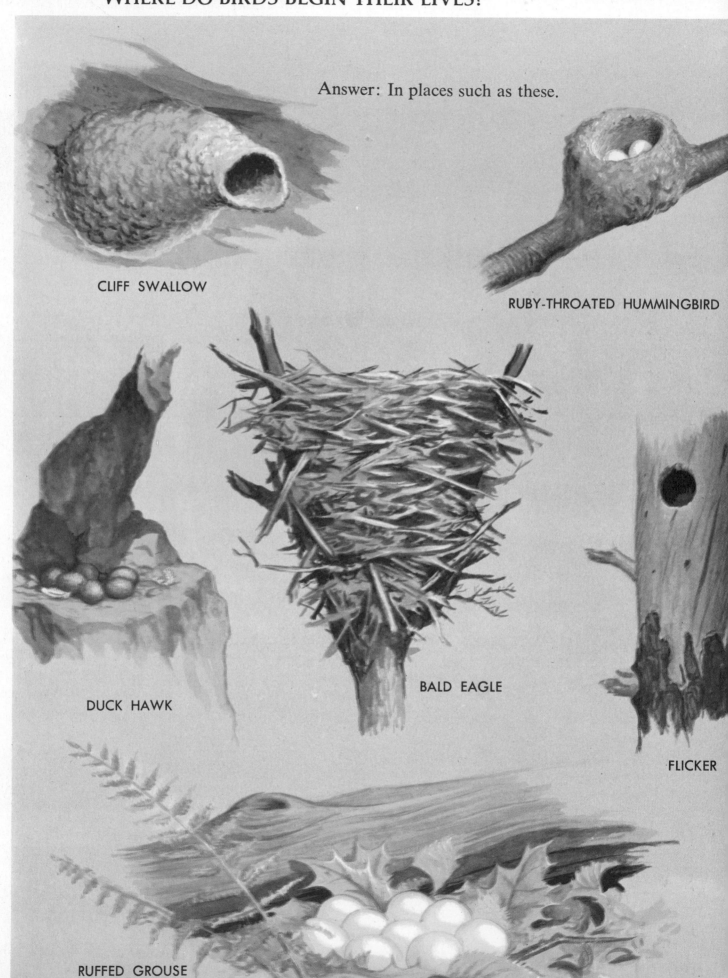

Answer: In places such as these.

CLIFF SWALLOW

RUBY-THROATED HUMMINGBIRD

DUCK HAWK

BALD EAGLE

FLICKER

RUFFED GROUSE

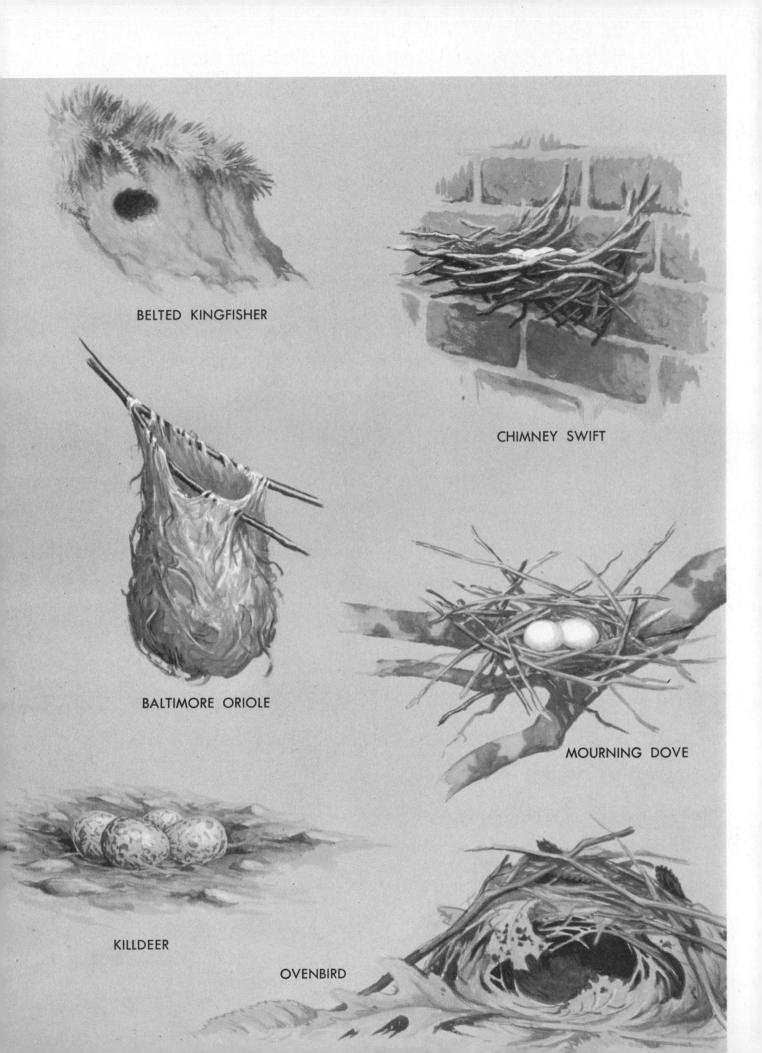

BELTED KINGFISHER

CHIMNEY SWIFT

BALTIMORE ORIOLE

MOURNING DOVE

KILLDEER

OVENBIRD

HOW DO BIRDS CONTROL THEIR FLIGHT?

A soaring eagle is a beautiful sight. It appears to be suspended from an invisible wire hooked in the clouds above. However, close watching through binoculars will show that even though the bird appears to be lazily gliding, it is actually very active. Its outer wing feathers (primaries) and tail feathers are in constant motion, catching updrafts of warm air, and steering the bird through these ever-moving air currents. By showing these large upward moving columns of warm air as (A), and their neighboring downdrafts of cooler air as (B), we can understand more easily how eagles, vultures, hawks, gulls and other soaring birds stay aloft.

Like other objects which are heavier than air, birds in flight are constantly falling. When a bird is in an updraft of warm air (A) it is carried up more quickly than it falls. At this time, it can gain altitude. The

The bird on the wing: A step-by-step picture sequence of a white stork taking off and rising on warm air.

bird now tries to keep itself in this column of air by steering with its wing and tail feathers. When the bird moves into the column of downward moving air (B) it falls rapidly. However, it now uses its wings to help it glide as quickly as possible into another column of upward-moving warm air (A). The speed that the bird attained while gliding downward in the "cool column" enables it to sweep upward more quickly when it enters the "warm column."

Flight is not confined to birds alone. Insects; fish (flying fish); frogs (Borneo flying frogs); snakes (Malayan flying snake); mammals (bats, phalangers, squirrels) have also taken to the air. However, there is no doubt that birds are the best fliers.

WHAT HELPS BIRDS FLY?

A bird watcher soon learns to identify birds by their flight. The wavy course of the flicker, the upswept darting of the goldfinch and the soaring of the marsh hawk are as different as the sizes and shapes of these birds.

Feathers, which evolved from the body scales of reptile ancestors, are an important part of the birds' flying equipment. They are strong and light in weight. Along the sides of the feathers are barbs which, if separated, look like fringe, or the branched ends which stick out from a piece of cloth. Each barb ends in a hook, which makes it possible for the barbs to hook on to one another. In this way a strong but very light flying wing is formed.

Internally, birds have air sacs and hollow bones which weigh less than solid flesh and bone. With less weight, birds fly better. Even their streamlined form is ideally shaped for flight.

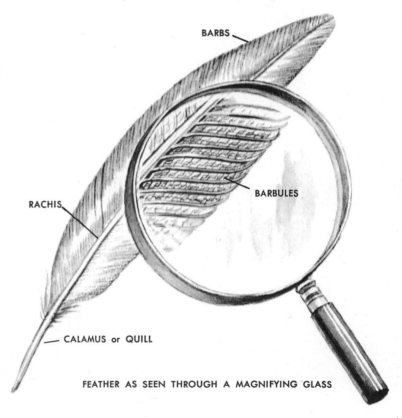

BARBS

BARBULES

RACHIS

CALAMUS or QUILL

FEATHER AS SEEN THROUGH A MAGNIFYING GLASS

WHAT TYPES OF BEAKS DO BIRDS HAVE?

Nature has provided birds with various types of bills, or beaks, which serve as instruments or means for gathering materials, making nests, and most especially for hunting and eating their daily food in a native environment. Flamingos, for example, are able to strain out mud from the plants and shellfish that are the mainstay of their diet by means of fine combs along the edges of their bills. Sparrows, finches and grosbeaks have exceptionally strong bills which can crack the hard shells of seeds

THE MAIN FEATHER TRACTS OF THE WING

SECONDARIES

COVERTS

PRIMARIES

FEATHERS OF MANY COLORS AND FORMS

BILLS FOR:

CRUSHING

TEARING

PROBING

SKIMMING

LEGS AND FEET FOR:

PERCHING

RUNNING

SWIMMING

quite easily. Woodpeckers use their beaks, which are shaped like chisels, to cut out nesting holes in trees or to get at insects. Brown creepers have long slender bills—a probing beak—which can pluck tree insects from cracks in the bark in the same way that tweezers are used. The heron has a long spearlike beak and the roseate spoonbill has a spoonlike beak.

WHAT TYPES OF FEET DO BIRDS HAVE?

Again, Nature provides in its own special way, according to the habitat in which a bird may find itself. Webbed feet are the "oars" or "paddles" which ducks and loons use to move swiftly through the water. Sharp curved claws, or talons, are used by hawks and owls to catch mice or small animals and carry them away. Woodpeckers have sharp claws for clutching and climbing the bark of trees. The songbirds, or perching birds, are able to stand on a branch by means of three toes in front (on each leg) and one in back.

WHAT TYPES OF BIRD FLIGHT ARE THERE?

There are four types of bird flight: *flapping, dynamic soaring, static soaring* and *gliding*. We have already mentioned static soaring and gliding.

Dynamic soaring is used by birds like the albatross and pelican. By heading into the wind, they use the force of the moving air to carry them up. After they have attained sufficient height or when the wind slackens, they glide quickly downward, gaining the forward speed necessary to reach new winds.

Flapping is the most complicated type of flight. All birds fly in this manner at some time, especially during takeoff. At this time, the hand part of the wing (the end which has primary feathers) is used to propel air backward, and in this way the bird gets a forward push. While the wings appear to be going straight up and down, they are really going in a some-what circular fashion. When the wing is lifted and brought forward, the primary feathers separate and allow air to pass between them. On the downstroke the feathers close tightly together, forming a flat wing surface which forces the air backward. The part of the wing nearest the body (the arm) does not move as much as the outer part (the hand), and is used by the bird as a lifting surface, like the wing of an airplane.

WHAT IS THE BEST-KNOWN NORTH AMERICAN BIRD?

Perhaps no bird is better known than the robin. People in the United States, Canada, and even Alaska are familiar with this rather plump ten-inch bird with its gray back and rusty red breast. It is a member of the thrush family, which includes the beautiful bluebird and the sweet-singing wood thrush. Its clear flutelike song is heard every morning, rain or shine, sounding as if it were happy to be alive.

The true robin, a smaller bird of similar coloring living in Europe, was so loved by the early English settlers that they gave its name to this American bird.

There is always something happening in the life of a robin, and it is an interesting bird to watch. It hops across the lawn or field, stopping every few feet, cocks its head to one side, and closely examines the ground for the hapless grub or insect that may be there. After a heavy rain the robin can often be seen tugging at one end of a large night crawler—an earthworm—which is trying desperately to escape down its burrow.

DO ROBINS ANNOUNCE SPRING?

Many people make the mistake of saying that spring is here as soon as they see a robin. It is true that most robins go south to warmer weather when it gets cold, but some robins stay north throughout the winter, finding their food on elderberry, sumac, mulberry and other bushes.

AMERICAN ROBIN

EUROPEAN ROBIN

A bright spring morning is the best time to hear the European robin (left) and the American robin (right).

DO ALL BIRDS GO SOUTH IN WINTER?

Not all bird migrations are north and south. Some birds, like the beautiful Australian birds of paradise, fly east and west. The slate-colored juncos in Tennessee move from a mountain top to the valley below. These birds also may be moving to a more abundant food supply.

The most remarkable migration is the trip made by the Arctic tern. This fifteen-inch gray bird, with a forked tail, red bill and black cap, flies each year from the Arctic to the Antarctic and back, traveling a distance of over 25,000 miles. It breeds in the Arctic, laying its eggs in a nest built of twigs, and it winters in the Antarctic, the home of the penguin.

ARE STARLINGS USEFUL BIRDS?

Starlings were brought to the United States from Europe in 1870. When first introduced, these birds showed a preference for living in the fields and woodlands and their food was mainly insects. However, they soon found an abundance of suitable food in fruit orchards and in the refuse of human communities. They began crowding out the house sparrow.

Starlings were first brought to the U.S. from Europe.

Because of their great numbers, they have become a problem in many cities. They roost by the thousands on the window ledges and masonry of large buildings, and their droppings spoil the looks of these places. Being large and quarrelsome permits them to steal the nesting sites of other birds. They also steal the songs of other birds. They are fine mimics, and often you will hear the notes of a robin or song sparrow coming from a tree, only to discover that the owner of the voice is a starling that has borrowed the tune.

However, not everything about this bird is bad. It still is a handsome creature and the amount of good it does by eating insects outweighs the damage it does to fruit crops.

WHICH IS THE WORLD'S LARGEST BIRD FAMILY?

Thirty-five or more different species of sparrows found in the United States are members of the world's largest family of birds, which includes more than six hundred kinds.

The European house sparrow, sometimes called the English sparrow, is really not a sparrow at all, but a weaver bird that has lived close to man for hundreds of years. The birds were brought from England to the eastern United States in 1850, with the hope that they would eat the many caterpillars which were then stripping the leaves from trees. Within a few years these birds were so numerous that they had spread across the country, becoming a serious pest and crowding out many native birds.

Most of the native sparrows are colored in somewhat the same soft tones of brown, tan and black. The fat little fox sparrow has rusty colored breast stripes and reddish cheek patches. The roly-poly chipping sparrow has a white throat and breast, brown wings and red topknot. Both birds have colors and patterns which make them attractive.

The actual size of the chipping sparrow is shown in the illustration. Chippies, as they are called, sing faster as the weather gets warmer. They eat seeds.

FOX SPARROW

TREE SPARROW

SAVANNA SPARROW

CAN SPARROWS SING?

The swamp, song, white-throat, ipswich, seaside, lark and tree sparrows are all talented songsters. But no more sweet and sprightly tune is heard outdoors than that of the song sparrow. It starts with three short, strong calls and is followed by a variety of notes which always end so quickly that one feels the sparrow didn't have time to finish its song.

WHAT DO SPARROWS EAT?

Most sparrows eat seeds, often feeding upon the food that man has grown for himself. However, a great part of their diet is made up of insects, particularly during the nesting season, when both parents carry insects to feed their young. Their love for seeds brings these birds close to our homes, and many different kinds visit the back yard, neighboring lot or field. Unlike the house sparrows, which build their nests close to human habitation, the true sparrows nest in the woodlands.

WHY DO BIRDS MOLT?

All birds shed their feathers (a process called *molting*), and grow a new set at least once a year. Some birds go through this process twice. During the molting period, some species are awkward and unable to defend themselves. These birds seek hiding places and live quietly until their "suit" is completed. If molting did not take place, the feathers would soon look very seedy and the bird would be unable to fly.

FLICKER

TUFTED TITMOUSE

BLUEJAY

HOODED WARBLER

CANADA WARBLER

MAGNOLIA WARBLER

BLACK-THROATED WARBLER

PARULA WARBLER

WHO ARE THE "BUTTERFLIES OF THE BIRD WORLD"?

There are over one hundred different kinds of warblers in the United States, and they are all small, four to six inches long. Because of the great variety and brilliance of their coloring, they have been called "butterflies of the bird world." One of the most brilliant is the male eastern yellow warbler. Its yellow body with striped red breast is like a flash of sunlight as it darts in and out of the new green of spring growth.

The nests of warblers can be found from northern Canada to the southern United States. They are built of twigs, grass and moss, and are sometimes tied together with pieces of spider or caterpillar web.

Warblers are protected and encouraged to build their nests near fruit orchards. There they help the farmer by finding insects both for themselves and their young.

RED-CROWNED PARROT

KEEL-BILLED TOUCAN

BLUE-CROWNED CHLOROPHONIA

RED-LEGGED HONEY CREEPERS

WHAT BIRDS LIVE IN THE JUNGLE?

Some of the most unusual birds in the world are found in the jungles. The variety of pattern, color and habits is so great that many books have been written about them. Few of us may ever have the opportunity to visit the jungles of Australia to observe the colorful lyre bird with its gracefully curved tail feathers—or to the South American rain forests to see the gaudily colored red, black and white toucan, with its large bright orange beak tipped with ivory black. However, we all can go to the local library, zoo or museum, and there see and read about the wonders of the bird world native to the distant jungles.

GREAT CURASSOW

QUETZAL

TURQUOISE-BROWED MOTMOT

GREEN JAY

BOAT-BILLED HERON

CRIMSON-COLORED TANAGER

SUN BITTERN

GREAT HORNED OWL

SCREECH OWL

BARN OWL

PYGMY OWL

SNOWY OWL

WHOO-O-O ARE THESE BIRDS?

Owls are naturally birds of the forests, deserts and jungles, but some of them have taken up life in barns, church steeples and even in trees in the town park. They are found in many parts of the world, and their hoots, shrieks and calls can be heard in all seasons. Their night sight is keen, and they can hear exceptionally well. A twig broken underfoot is enough to warn them. With their sharp eyes and wings that make no sound in flight, they have become expert at catching rodents, rabbits, and other small mammals. The false belief that owls cannot see in the daytime probably comes from their inability to see unless the object is directly ahead of their eyes. To look to one side, they have to turn their heads in that direction, and they can actually see directly over their backs.

The great horned owl is slightly smaller than the snowy owl and lives in the deep forests of Canada and the United States. The abundance of rodents around human habitations often lures them to the woodlands near towns. They are easily recognized by the hornlike tufts of feathers growing from either side at the front of the head. They rarely build nests, but use those abandoned by hawks and crows.

The snowy owl of the Arctic, Canada and the northern United States is well camouflaged in snow. Occasionally it may be driven south by severe winter storms. These birds make their nests in the mountains above the tree line, usually in open, barren country. The nest is nothing more than a depression in the ground.

Burrowing owls, residents of the deserts of the Southwest, are ten inches tall. They do not build nests, but use the abandoned burrows of the prairie dog. Burrowing owls feed on grasshoppers and other insects, and small rodents. Unlike most other owls, they do their hunting in the daytime.

The burrowing owl prefers the nest of some ground mammal rather than any nest of its own construction.

ARE DUCKS AND GEESE RELATED?

Ducks can be found the world over. They are usually seen in flocks on freshwater ponds, lakes and swamps, and salt-water oceans, bays and inlets. The fondness for water is common to all of them, and they are able to swim rapidly because of a webbing of skin between their toes. They have oil glands on the body which provide a waterproof covering for their feathers. Those ducks that dive for their food are thus able to surface with dry wings, ready for flight on a moment's notice.

One of the most beautiful birds known is the eighteen-inch wood duck of the United States and Mexico. It is gaudily colored and unfortunately, the great beauty of these birds is a danger to them, because hunters seek them out as a prize. As many as twenty-four eggs are laid by the female in a nest in a hollow tree high off the ground.

Unlike the wood duck, the mallard builds its nest on the ground near a deep swamp, hidden by a dense growth of rushes and cattail plants. The nest is warmly lined with down feathers from the mother's breast.

These birds are of great economic importance. They are an excellent control for mosquitoes, which they catch in the larval stage (water form) of the insect's life cycle. Many farmers encourage the mallards' presence on the farm pond for this reason. They not only feed upon myriads of land insects, but they themselves are used by man as food. It is this duck, more than any other, that has been used for breeding purposes to produce many of the domesticated ducks used the world over.

Geese are merely larger ducks, with male and female similar in color and pattern. The males of the smaller ducks are usually "clothed" in brighter colors.

COMMON TERN

SPOONBILL

WHITE STORK

MOOR HEN

LITTLE GREBE

HERON

STILTS

BLACK TERN

MARBLED DUCK

RUDDY SHELDUCK

KENTISH PLOVERS

FERRUGINOUS DUCK

SANDPIPERS

SKIMMER

WHAT BIRDS ARE BEACH AND OCEAN BIRDS?

Many different kinds of birds find their food and homes near the beach. These include the skimmer, a bird which glides along a few inches above the ocean, using its lower bill to skim food from just below the surface of the water. Another is the sandpiper which races back and forth across the sand, catching sand fleas and other small crustaceans as they are exposed by the wash of the waves.

Most common of the beach birds are those we call sea gulls. There are many species of gulls and not all kinds are found near salt water. Some forms are found near inland waterways and lakes many hundreds of miles from the ocean. These birds are important to man because they feed upon refuse and carrion and thereby keep the beaches clean.

Herring gulls are, by far, the most common. They occur by the thousands along the coast, particularly near towns and cities. One of its most interesting habits is to take a clam—which has proven too hard to break—into the air, and drop it upon a stone in order to expose the meaty food inside.

A graceful white bird often seen from ships in the southern Pacific is the albatross. These are the largest of the ocean birds, with a wingspread that sometimes exceeds eleven feet. Their ability to soar on the constant winds over the ocean is exceeded by no other bird. Without a single wing beat they can fly for miles, sometimes gliding so close to the water that they momentarily disappear between the crests of the waves.

WHAT BIRD HAS ITS OWN FISHNET?

A brown pelican feeds its young from the pouch.

Along the coastal waters of southern California, Florida, the Gulf, and the Atlantic coasts of Central and South America is a bird whose lower mandible (beak) has a large fold of skin that serves as a net for catching fish. It is the brown pelican. Soaring above the water, it spies a fish, folds its wings, and dives into the water in pursuit. When it surfaces, it will push the water out of its distended pouch and swallow the captured fish whole.

These birds build their simple gravel and rubbish nests on small islands. Their one or two young receive food by placing their heads into the mother's gullet for recently captured fish which she has partially digested.

DO PENGUINS BUILD NESTS?

Even the land of ice and constant cold has its bird population. Penguins, the small flightless birds that stand upright and look like attentive waiters at a swank country club, are a prize exhibit at most zoos.

The nesting habits of the king penguin, a species that lives in desolate, cold regions, are interesting. They keep their eggs from freezing by carrying them between the belly and feet. The incubation period lasts seven weeks, during which time the eggs are transferred from the male to the female.

Penguins are good swimmers, and the fish they catch are the main part of their diet. Not all of the sixteen different kinds live in the Antarctic. One species actually lives at the equator, on the Galapagos Islands.

This is a colony of black-footed penguins.

RAVEN

COMMON CROW

HOW DO CROWS DIFFER FROM RAVENS?

The common raven of the old world, in northern United States and Canada, is twenty-six inches long and is the largest of the three all-black birds called crows. They live in the forests and on high cliffs along the coast. Ravens' nests are crude affairs constructed of strong sticks, lined with seaweed and grass, and built in the tops of tall pines or on rocks.

The well-known common crow is found throughout the United States and Mexico, and if seen alone is hard to distinguish from the raven. But the raven's voice, its larger size, and its wedge-shaped tail distinguish it from the crow. The call of the raven is a hoarse *cr-r-r-cruk* sound, while the call of the crow is a distinct *caw-caw-caw*.

Like ravens, crows build their nests high in the trees, but their nests are better constructed, being built of sticks and lined with strips of bark, vines, dry grass, leaves and moss. Outwardly they appear to be very rough, but the lining is snug and warm. The parents will often continue to feed their young even after the young have left the nest.

32

WHAT BIRD IS A "HELICOPTER BIRD"?

The hummingbird. These tiny birds are the best fliers in birdland, capable of flying straight up or down, forward or backward, or hovering in one spot for many minutes. Their short wings move so quickly that they appear to be merely a blur. They are at home in the fields, in the brush and in the forest, and can also be found near homes, particularly if honeysuckle or trumpet vine is growing nearby. Their extremely long beaks—almost one-fourth as long as the bird—are inserted into the bell-like flowers, and the tongue (which is a double-barreled tube) sucks up sweet nectar at the base of the flower. Hummingbirds also eat many small insects.

Small hummingbirds are often mistaken for large insects and sometimes a large bird will pursue them, perhaps thinking it is chasing a moth. However, hummingbirds are so quick in their flight that they soon outdistance the larger bird. This extraordinary skill in flying makes them unafraid, and they can occasionally be seen teasing larger birds by flying at them.

RUBY-THROATED HUMMINGBIRDS

SPARROW HAWK

DUCK HAWK

COOPER'S HAWK

SWALLOW-TAILED HA

CARACARA HAWK

ROUGH-LEGGED HA

WHICH BIRDS ARE HAWKS?

More than five hundred different forms of hawks inhabit many areas throughout the world. This large group includes the vultures, buzzards, eagles, falcons, hawks and kites. They are mainly birds of prey, catching and killing their food by striking it from the air and upon the ground.

Birds of this group actually perform a valuable service for man by feeding upon vast numbers of rodents and other destructive small mammals. Some species, such as Cooper's hawk and the sharp-shinned hawk, sometimes feed upon small fowl in unprotected farmyards.

Hawks vary greatly in size. The sparrow hawk is a small bird, about eight to ten inches long, which may be seen throughout the greater part of North America, as far south as Costa Rica. It seeks small prey.

The American duck hawk, found throughout most of North and South America, and its European counterpart are similar in appearance. It can overtake and capture any bird, except possibly the swift or the humming-bird. The hunting flight starts high in the sky. After attaining a high speed, the duck hawk half-folds its wings and moves so fast that the air can be heard rushing through its feathers. Its flight is under control at all times. If the prey swerves, the duck hawk quickly alters course. The force of the impact of being seized or struck by the powerful talons of the hawk renders the prey helpless. No other bird will try to pilfer a duck hawk's nest.

Eagles float on the air high above the ground, at times so far up that they appear as a mere speck against the blue. They have often been accused of swooping down and carrying off small children. These stories are untrue. Their food, mainly fish, is found dead on the beach, and sometimes stolen from smaller birds. If pressed by hunger, they will hunt for themselves. There are many accounts of eagles chasing and capturing ducks and geese. Eagles' nests (called eyries) are built of strong sticks on craggy cliff sides high above the ground.

The California condor (almost extinct), found in the mountains of Lower California, and the South American condor, are the largest birds that fly. They are approximately four and a half feet long and have a wingspread of eleven feet. The South American condor is found in the Andes Mountains and has been observed at altitudes of over 20,000 feet.

WHAT ARE FELINES?

The many kinds of cats in the world all belong to the group called *feline*, a name that comes from *felis*, the Latin word for "cat." All felines, except the domestic cat, are wild animals.

Felines are by nature carniverous, that is, flesh-eaters. Their canine teeth are longer and sharper than those of any other flesh-eating animal, and their other teeth are sharp, too. When a cat closes its jaws, the edges of the upper and lower teeth move past each other like the blade-edges of a pair of shears. Such teeth easily cut through tough flesh, cartilage and sinew. They can also crack bones, but felines do not have special bone-crushing teeth as some other flesh-eating animals do.

A feline's claws are sharper than those of any other mammal. They are hook-shaped and end in needlelike points. The claws are attached to muscles that enable a cat to extend the claws or to pull them back into sheaths in its paws. A feline's teeth and claws give it the most dreaded weapons of any animal its size.

WHY DO CATS' EYES SHINE IN THE DARK?

You may have seen the coppery-green glare of a cat's eyes at night. This glare is due to the reflection of light from a substance called *guanin* that lines the inside of a cat's eyes. The purpose of this substance, however, is not to cause a cat's eyes to shine. Guanin intensifies whatever light enters a cat's eyes and enables the animal to see objects in almost pitch darkness. A cat cannot see in complete darkness.

WHY DO CATS HAVE WHISKERS?

Felines have very acute hearing. Not only can they hear very faint sounds, but they can also detect other vibrations of the air. When these slight air movements reach certain hairs in a cat's ears, the contact is transmitted to nerves at the roots of the hairs. Thus the cat is made aware of nearby movements that are even too slight to produce sounds or to catch its eye. A cat's whiskers serve exactly the same purpose as the hairs in its ears, and thus the whiskers are delicate sense organs.

The sense of touch in a cat is one of the most delicate in the world. Besides being able to "feel" with its whiskers, a cat can feel with every hair on its body. Notice, for example, the first reaction of a cat when you start to pet it. It will seemingly recoil from the touch, because the hair has transmitted a natural "warning."

Felines stalk their prey. Most cats can run fast for only very short distances, and so they must move close to their intended victims before launching a final attack. A hunting cat, with claws pulled into the sheaths, moves silently on padded feet. When it has approached fairly close to its prey, the cat flattens itself upon the ground and creeps forward on its belly. Now and then it makes short, silent dashes from one place of concealment to the next. When the cat has finally crept within springing distance, it leaps upon its prey.

The common domestic cat that is regularly fed by people probably does not stalk mice or birds to get itself a meal, but rather to "play the game" of "catch" in obeying its natural hunting instinct. Sometimes the  tables are turned. During the nesting season, bluejays have been seen to attack a marauding cat by flying at its head and pecking until the cat decided it would be happier elsewhere.

WHICH ARE THE BIGGEST CATS?

Tigers are the biggest cats of Asia. They may be found in areas from the steaming jungles of southern India and Malaya to the snowy forests of Siberia. The average tiger is about nine feet long, measured from the nose to the tip of the tail. It stands about three feet high and weighs more than 400 pounds. Siberian tigers may reach a length of thirteen feet and a weight of 650 pounds.

The fur of southern tigers is short and glossy. It ranges in color from yellow to red-orange and has black stripes. The fur of tigers that live in Siberia, the Caucasus and northern Korea is a creamy yellow with dark brown stripes. Since tigers dwell in jungles and forests, their striped coats make them difficult to see among the shadows of trees and bushes. The highly colored fur of the southern tigers blends with the colors of dead leaves in the jungle, while the light fur of the northern tigers blends with the snow.

HOW LONG DOES A TIGER LIVE?

There are usually two or three tiger kittens in a litter, each of which weighs a little more than two pounds. Their eyes are closed and do not open until the kittens are two weeks old. The mother tiger takes very good care of her kittens. She nurses them until they are able to eat meat and fiercely protects them from enemies. Until they are about six months old, the kittens spend most of their time in play. After that, the mother tiger begins to teach them how to hunt. When they are about a year old, the young tigers are able to shift for themselves. A wild tiger lives about fifteen years, but some in zoos have lived more than twenty years.

A tiger is an Asian member of the cat family.

Skull of a typical carnivore.

LEOPARD

WHAT IS A CARNIVORE?

Flesh-eating animals live by devouring other animals. Because of this, they are unusually savage, quick and strong for their size. The scientific name for flesh-eater is *carnivore*, from the Latin words *carnis*, meaning "flesh," and *vorare*, meaning "to devour." Carnivores use their sharp claws and long, sharp teeth to catch and tear the prey they hunt. In each of their upper and lower jaws are two teeth that are longer than the rest—the *canine teeth*—and all flesh-eaters have them. The Latin word for dog is *canis*, and canine teeth were so named because of their presence in dogs. The carnivores' main diet is flesh, though many, including bears and raccoons, also eat fruits, berries and other plant foods.

BEAR PAW

There are many kinds of carnivores throughout the world, including leopards, tigers, lynxes, weasels and members of the weasel family. Raccoons and members of the raccoon family are also carnivorous. These include the pandas, kinkajous and coatis. Other flesh-eating animals are the fur-bearing minks, martens, sables and wolverines. The snake-killing mongoose, the scavenging hyena, civet cats and all felines are some of the many other carnivores.

LION PAW

A tiger's normal diet consists of deer, antelope and wild pigs—animals that seriously damage farmers' crops in the Far East. Many tigers, however, prey on domestic cattle and some have stalked humans. These are the so-called "man-eaters." Man-eating tigers are old or crippled animals. When a tiger becomes old, its teeth wear down and its claws split and become dull. In this condition, the tiger finds it very difficult to kill its normal prey. It may then turn to human beings, a prey that is very easy to stalk and kill.

FOX PAW

Tigers have an appetite for porcupine flesh, but they sometimes get porcupine quills in their paws which may work their way up the tiger's leg and cripple the animal. These crippled tigers may then turn to killing people. One tiger that had killed more than a hundred persons was found to have more than thirty porcupine quills in its flesh.

WEASEL PAW

Sometimes a young, healthy tiger becomes a man-eater. Some hunters believe that the mother of such a tiger was a man-eater and taught her cub to kill humans. Most tigers, however, avoid people.

RACCOON PAW

OTTER PAW

WHAT IS A LAUGHING HYENA?

A hyena can make a remarkably wide range of sounds. Its usual cry begins on a low mournful note and rises to a shrill climax. It barks and growls and can imitate the roar of a lion. When a hyena finds a carcass, it sends out a weird cry that sounds like an insane human laugh, which has earned it the nickname of "laughing hyena."

Hyenas range the plains of Africa, the Middle East and India looking for dead animals. They have exceptionally large teeth and powerful jaws that help them crack the bones of larger animals, such as zebras and buffaloes. Despite this powerful armament, the hyena avoids fighting with other animals. Even when cornered, it will try to escape rather than fight its way to freedom. It may play dead when attacked; then, when the attacker turns its attention away for a moment, the hyena leaps up and runs away.

Many people call the hyena a coward because of these characteristics. But such labels are meaningless, for we cannot judge pride, bravery and courage in a hyena by human standards. It is a natural characteristic for this animal to save itself in the face of danger by running away or faking death.

The hyena has a broad head with bulging eyes and stubby ears. Its thick neck is topped by a sparse mane of stiff hairs, and its gray fur, splotched with brown or black spots, gives the hyena a mangy appearance.

Its belly sags, and the hind legs, shorter than the forelegs, cause the hyena's body to slope downward from the shoulders to the short tail.

HYENA FAMILY

SPOTTED HYENA

STRIPED HYENA

WHY DO RACCOONS WASH THEIR FOOD?

Raccoons, while they also eat nuts and fruit, are considered flesh-eaters. They prey on birds, fish, frogs, snails, snakes and other animals. They live in most parts of the United States, make their home near water and are good swimmers. Raccoons wash their food to make it soft. Their fur, for which they are hunted, is still in demand. These animals make good pets. The coati, or coati-mondi, is a South American relative of the raccoon.

RACCOON FAMILY

COATI

RACCOON

WEASEL

FERRET

WEASEL FAMILY

MARTEN

OTTER

WHO ARE THE WEASELS?

The members of the weasel family, important to man because of their fur, are found all over the world except in Australia and New Guinea. Some other members of the weasel family are the marten, mink, badger, skunk, otter and ferret. The black-footed ferret, the largest of the North American weasels, may grow about two feet long.

41

WHAT IS A WILD ANIMAL?

A wild animal is one that lives entirely without the aid and care of man. It does not depend on man for either food or protection. A tiger in a jungle, a rabbit in a field, a polar bear on the Arctic ice—all are wild animals. If you think carefully about this definition, you will see that any living thing that is not a plant and is not taken care of by man is a wild animal. This would include a fish, an oyster in the sea, insects and even the tiny one-celled animals that we can see only under a microscope.

WHAT IS A MAMMAL?

The word "mammal" comes from the Latin word *mamma,* which means breast. All mammals nurse their young with milk produced by the mother animal's breasts or *mammary glands.* Another thing almost all mammals have in common is that their young are born alive.

Shown are a red fox and cubs near their den.

All mammals have hair or fur covering their skin. Some, including whales, armadillos and elephants, have very few hairs. All mammals have four limbs—a pair of forelimbs and a pair of hind limbs. In most mammals the four limbs are legs. Some mammals move about only on their hind limbs. In some mammals the limbs are flippers used for swimming, while in others, one pair of limbs has become wings.

Mammals have sharp senses. Sight, hearing, smell and touch are well developed in these animals. Most have one or two senses that are keener than the rest. Tigers, for example, have very sharp ears and eyes which enable them to locate and stalk their prey in the jungle. But their sense of smell is only fair. The senses that best enable each kind of mammal to find food and escape its enemies are much keener than its other senses.

TREE PORCUPINE

GRASSHOPPER MOUSE

GRAY SQUIRREL

PRAIRIE DOG

HARE

WHO ARE THE GNAWING MAMMALS?

There are more members in the group of gnawing mammals than in any other group of mammals. Among them are mice, rats, squirrels, chipmunks, beavers, porcupines, guinea pigs, prairie dogs, chinchillas, rabbits and hares. All except the last two are called *rodents*.

The two front teeth in the upper and lower jaws of rodents are long, flat and sharp. The inner surface of these teeth has no enamel and is constantly being worn down, so that the teeth always have sharp, chisel-like edges.

WHO ARE THE FLYING MAMMALS?

The bat is the only mammal that has wings. Its wings are made of membrane and are supported by the bones of its forelimbs. The wings are attached to the body from the shoulders down to the lower part of the hind limbs. The "thumb" of a bat's forelimb is free from the wing membrane and bears a hooked claw with which the animal hangs from perches when it is resting. Bats range in size from the so-called flying foxes that are a foot long to the inch-long species.

The more than two thousand known kinds of bats may be divided into two main branches: the fruit-eaters and the insect-eaters. Bats also eat fish, meat, nectar and blood. Bats drink water by skimming it from the surface while they are in flight.

DO BATS FOLLOW PEOPLE?

Bats sometimes follow people walking outdoors at night. If you are taking a walk some evening and one or two bats flit about your head, they are probably little brown, or mouse-eared, bats that are picking off mosquitos following you. They are not trying to get into your hair, as some misinformed people still believe. The little brown bat has to devour half its weight in insects every night just to survive.

WHAT IS A VAMPIRE BAT?

Vampire bats live in the tropical Americas and drink the blood of mammals, including man. The vampire bat is three inches long and has razor-sharp front teeth with which it attacks its victims. Actually, very little blood is lost from such a bite and the cut heals easily. However, vampire bats transmit diseases, including rabies, which may infect man and destroy fowl and other livestock.

Over the years, many legends and superstitions about the bat—especially the vampire bat—have developed. Tales about human beings turning into bats or evil vampires are quite imaginative, of course, but untrue.

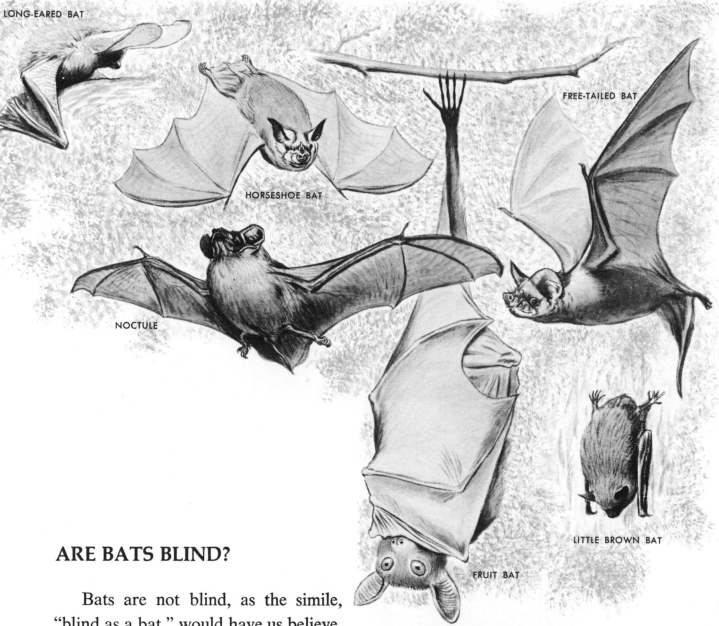

LONG-EARED BAT

HORSESHOE BAT

FREE-TAILED BAT

NOCTULE

LITTLE BROWN BAT

FRUIT BAT

ARE BATS BLIND?

Bats are not blind, as the simile, "blind as a bat," would have us believe. They have perfectly good eyes that are hidden in thick fur. But for centuries men have been puzzled by bats' extremely skillful flight. As they hunt for insects on the wing at night, bats zoom and dive among the branches of trees, yet never collide into them, even in pitch darkness. In the eighteenth century, an Italian scientist named Lazzaro Spallanzani proved that a bat's flight is not directed by sight.

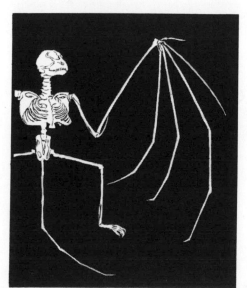

The skeleton of a bat shows the long bones in the "wing," which may be compared to the fingers of the human hand.

HOW CAN BATS "FLY BLIND"?

The answer was provided not too many years ago. It was learned that bats navigate by means of a system of natural radar. In radar, radio waves broadcast from a radar station strike a moving object—an airplane, for example—and are reflected back to the radar station. Here the reflected waves reveal the location of the plane. As a bat flies along, it emits sound waves too high for the human ear to hear. The echoes of these sound waves, bouncing off obstacles ahead, return to the bat's ears. (In some species, the echo returns to a fleshy ridge around the bat's lips and muzzle.) Upon receiving the reflected sound waves, the bat is made aware of the object ahead. The sound that bats use for their "radar" should not be confused with their high-pitched squeak. The "radar" sound is a steady hum.

WHO ARE THE EGG-LAYING MAMMALS?

All mammals, except one kind, bear their young alive. This exceptional group of mammals has only two members; the echidna, or spiny anteater, and the duckbill platypus. These animals lay eggs from which their young hatch. Both have birdlike beaks. Both nurse their young with milk, but neither has nipples from which the milk can flow. Instead, the milk comes out of small pores in the abdomen of the animals. The young then lap up the milk. These animals are found in Australia, Tasmania, New Zealand and New Guinea.

The spiny anteater has short, sharp spines among its brownish gray fur. It has powerful digging claws on all four feet and can burrow into the earth at amazing speed. It does not dig down head-first, but with all four feet digging at once, it sinks into the ground. When attacked, it will burrow underground, exposing only a spiny back with which no attacker wants to come in contact.

The spiny anteater

At the left is a duckbill platypus in the water. It is an expert swimmer. At the right, a platypus nurses its young.

The duckbill platypus is an expert swimmer. It has grayish brown fur that is close and thick, webbed feet, long claws and a flat tail. Unlike the spiny anteater, it has teeth and eats worms, tadpoles and small fish. The female platypus digs a den in the bank of a stream in preparation for her young. A tunneled entrance to this large chamber is under water; there is also an air shaft to the surface. The den, in which there are two or three eggs, is lined with leaves and grass. The thin-shelled eggs are about the size of a marble and are stuck together side by side. The mother platypus holds the eggs to her breast and rolls herself into a ball to provide warmth for hatching. Baby platypuses are hairless and blind. It takes about four months before they can see.

On each hind foot of a male platypus is a sharp, horny, hollow spur connected to a poison gland. A slash from this spur can cause a painful wound.

HATCHING PLATYPUS

WHAT ARE MARSUPIALS?

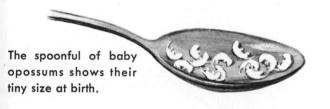

The spoonful of baby opossums shows their tiny size at birth.

Marsupials get their name from the Latin word meaning "pouch," because most female marsupials have pouches in which to carry their young. Kangaroos and opossums are two examples of this kind of animal. Newborn marsupials are extremely small when compared to the adults. A newborn kangaroo, for example, is only an inch long, and twenty newborn opossums can fit into a tablespoon.

WHAT DOES "PLAYING POSSUM" MEAN?

Opossums are the only marsupials, or pouched mammals, in North America, of which the Virginia opossum is the best known. It is gray-white in color and about the size of a house cat. This animal is slow in its movements and its sharp teeth and claws do not provide an effective defense against enemies. Its feet have "thumbs" that enable the opossum to hold objects in the same way that a human hand does. Its ratlike tail is prehensile; that is, it can be used to grasp objects, such as a tree branch, from which the opossum is often found suspended.

When confronted with danger, an opossum suffers so great a shock that it falls into a deathlike coma. In this state, it can be struck, pinched and poked with sharp objects without responding. As a result, some of its attackers may leave it for dead. When the danger is past, the animal revives and flees. This behavior is known as "playing possum."

An opossum has many natural enemies, including hawks, owls and foxes. Man also hunts the opossum because it is destructive to poultry and eggs. Its flesh is also considered a delicacy in some areas and its fur is valuable. But the opossum also destroys insects and harmful rodents.

WHAT HAPPENS TO BABY OPOSSUMS?

A female opossum may bear as many as twenty bee-sized young each year, even though not all of them survive. Opossums are hairless, blind and not completely developed at birth. However, they are able to crawl into their mother's pouch. There each one attaches itself to a nipple and the helpless animals suckle for almost two months. Some of the newborn opossums cannot reach the pouch, and these starve. Five to sixteen young are nursed, and afterward, they climb on their mother's back, where they are carried for several weeks. The young opossums are shaken loose when the mother feels that they can take care of themselves.

The baby opossums spend their first three months in their mother's pouch. Afterward, they ride on the mother's back.

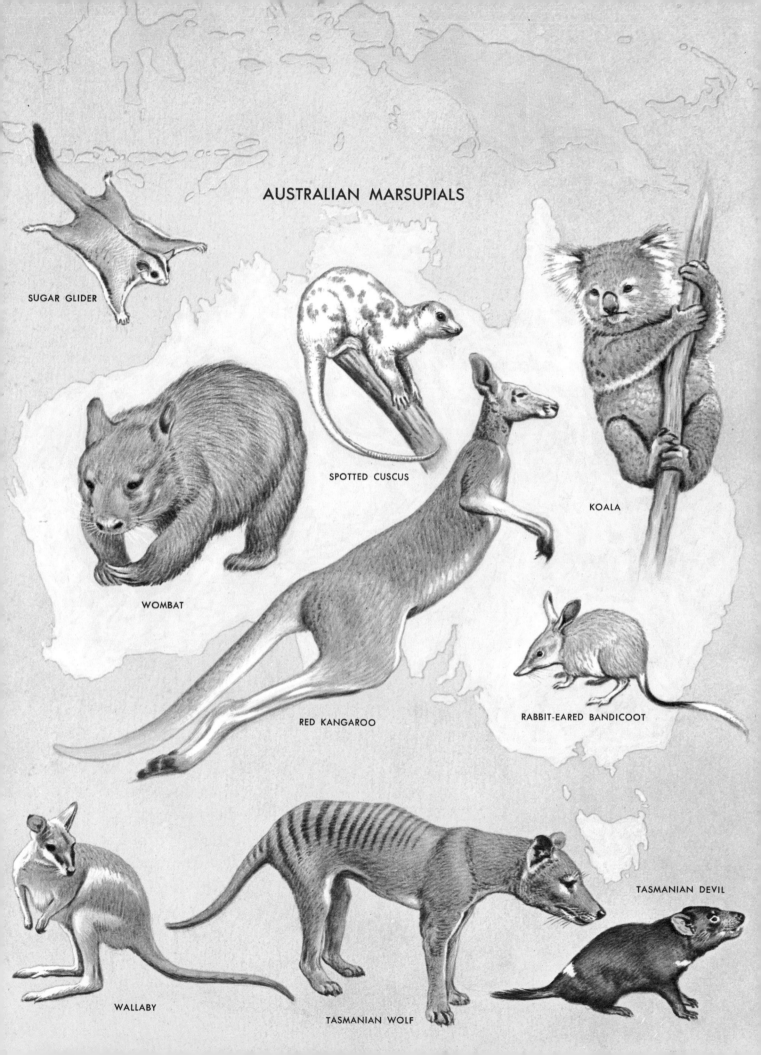

AUSTRALIAN MARSUPIALS

SUGAR GLIDER

SPOTTED CUSCUS

KOALA

WOMBAT

RED KANGAROO

RABBIT-EARED BANDICOOT

TASMANIAN DEVIL

WALLABY

TASMANIAN WOLF

WHAT ANIMALS TRADE BABIES?

The koala looks like a teddy bear with big ears and a shiny nose. It has small, bright eyes and a puzzled expression.

The mother koala has only one baby at a time. At birth, it is only about an inch long and no fatter than a lead pencil. It takes six months before the baby's eyes open and it can climb out of its mother's pouch. For another whole year, the mother koala carries her growing baby with her. Sometimes, when several mothers and their offspring have been wandering about together in the trees, the babies may become temporarily separated from their parents. If this happens at nursing time, it is not unusual for some koala mothers to nurse the young of other koalas. After the meal, the babies return to their own mothers.

The koala lives in Australia. Because it looks like a bear, it has also been called the pouched bear, teddy bear and Australian bear.

HOW DID THE KANGAROO GET ITS NAME?

Kangaroos have very large hind limbs upon which they stand upright and use for hopping and leaping. They use their long, powerful tails to balance themselves when standing, and it gives them an extra push when jumping. These marsupials were given their name by the famous eighteenth-century English explorer, Captain James Cook. Pointing to one of the animals, he asked an Australian native what it was called. "Kangaroo," replied the man, which, in his native language, meant "I don't know."

There are many kinds of kangaroos and these vary in size. The wallaby, for example, is no bigger than a rabbit, while the great kangaroo, or forester, stands seven feet tall and weighs two hundred pounds. The remarkable fact is that the newborn young of the larger species are only about an inch long.

Kangaroos often gather in herds called "mobs." In Australia's early days, such mobs numbered thousands of kangaroos; nowadays, a mob of one hundred animals is unusually large. Kangaroos lie down on the ground to sleep. Their diet consists mainly of vegetable matter. This marsupial's average life expectancy is fifteen years. Normally, a kangaroo hops from five to ten feet with each leap; but when it is in a hurry, it increases the length of each hop to fifteen or twenty feet. Circus trainers sometimes teach kangaroos to box, using boxing gloves. The animals frequently become quite adept in their circus performances.

WHO ARE THE SEA MAMMALS?

Not all mammals live on land. Some live in the sea, and these include whales, dolphins and porpoises. Millions of years ago, though, the ancestors of these sea mammals did live on land and crawled about on four limbs. Some adapted themselves to a life in the sea. Gradually, their forelimbs developed into flippers and their hind limbs shrank and disappeared into their bodies.

The mammals that live in the seas or in bays and rivers are warm-blooded, while all the other animals that live in water are cold-blooded. This means that the blood of these mammals—as in all other mammals—remains at a constant temperature. Whether the water is warm or cold, the temperature of the sea-living mammals remains the same. However, the body temperature of other animals in the sea changes to the temperature of the water in which they live.

WHAT IS THE LARGEST ANIMAL?

The largest animal known is the sulphur-bottom whale, which may measure over a hundred feet in length and weigh as much as 300,000 pounds. These animals, also called blue whales, are larger than the giant dinosaurs that lived millions of years ago.

The sulphur-bottom whale, or blue whale, is the largest animal in the world. It swims about 25 miles an hour.

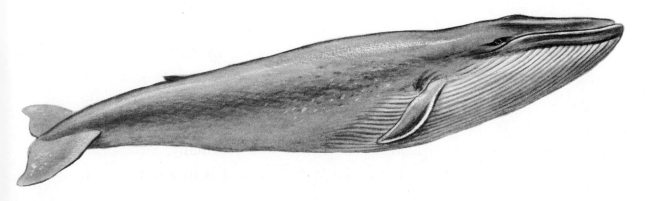

WHO ARE THE CANINES?

A group of wild animals resembling the domestic dog, which includes coyotes, wolves, jackals, wild dogs and foxes, are known as canines. The resemblance is accountable, inasmuch as they have all descended from common prehistoric ancestors. Canines are carnivores (flesh-eaters), but some will also eat fruits and vegetables. They have long muzzles and powerful jaws. In addition to the four canine teeth that are used to hold prey, they have flat teeth for crushing bones, and shearing teeth for cutting.

Wild canines have bushy tails. They have slender legs, and although they might not be as fast as some other animals in running, they have great endurance. Their erect ears can be moved to point in the direction from which a sound is coming. They also have good eyesight (although they are color-blind). But their best-developed sense is smell.

Canines have fairly sharp claws that are always extended. (Unlike cats' paws, they cannot be pulled into sheaths.) And when these doglike animals are overheated, their tongues hang out, because they perspire through glands in their tongues.

ARE COYOTES HARMFUL ANIMALS?

The early pioneers who brought their livestock west of the Mississippi River soon learned that coyotes would attack sheep, goats, chickens and geese, and thus coyotes came to be despised. But coyotes also prey on harmful rodents, so it is an undecided question as to whether coyotes do more harm than good. A campaign against coyotes in a western state was once so effective that these animals nearly disappeared, but in the next few years prairie dogs did so much crop damage that coyotes were allowed to return. Formerly, the coyote could be seen only in the central and western parts of the United States, but continued harassment has caused them to move to some eastern states and Canada.

A coyote is a slender, graceful animal about four feet long, standing about twenty-two inches high at the shoulder, and weighing twenty to thirty pounds. It has a gray or tawny coat of long, soft fur that is white on its underside. One-third of its length is a bushy tail tipped with black.

Illustrated here are some of the foremost members of the canine group. They show all the physical features that have given them the name of "doglike" mammals.

COYOTE

ARCTIC FOX

WOLF

CAPE HUNTING DOG

FENNEC

RED FOX

WHY DO COYOTES PLAY DEAD?

The coyote is a very clever animal. Mexicans think so highly of a coyote's intelligence that when they want to describe someone who is very crafty, they say he is "muy coyote"—very coyote-like. In their spread to the eastern states, coyotes have adapted themselves to living around thickly populated areas—even to eating vegetables and garbage. One wildlife officer has said that coyotes can pick out the best watermelons in a patch. Sometimes a coyote will play dead to catch carrion-eating birds—birds that eat dead-animal flesh.

Coyotes never attack men and, if caught young, make excellent pets.

AFRICAN ELEPHANT

WHAT ARE THE TWO KINDS OF ELEPHANTS?

The elephant is the largest and most powerful of all land animals. It may stand thirteen feet high and weigh six tons. Elephants are among the most intelligent of animals. They easily learn to do many kinds of work as well as circus tricks, and they show concern for each other's well-being.

There are two kinds of elephants—the African and the Indian. The bush elephant of Africa is larger. It averages eleven feet at the shoulder, weighs about five tons and is darker than its Indian cousin. It also has larger ears and a more sloping forehead. It likes shade, and therefore lives in the thick bush or in forests. This huge animal uses its enormous ears, which are more than a yard wide, as fans. An elephant has good hearing, but its sense of smell is probably the sharpest of any animal.

The Indian elephant is smaller than the bush elephant. It averages nine feet in height and three-and-a-half tons in weight. This animal is more easily tamed and trained than its African cousin. It has done heavy labor for the people of southern Asia for centuries. When the Indian elephant sleeps, it usually lies down; the African elephant usually sleeps upright.

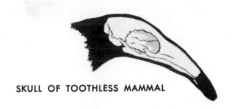

WHO ARE THE TOOTHLESS MAMMALS?

Among a group of toothless mammals are the armadillos. They are found in tropical South America, Central America and the southern United States. The armadillo's body is covered by an armor of bony plates. When attacked, the animal can tuck its head and feet under this horny shell and roll up into a ball. Some animals, of course, can smash the protective cover with their paws, but many of the armadillo's natural enemies find the armor too tough to grip.

Armadillos can burrow into the ground very quickly with the aid of their powerful claws. They feed on ants, termites and other insects which they catch on their long, sticky tongues. The largest armadillo is about three feet long; the smallest is about five inches in length. Many people eat its flesh, and the Indians once made baskets out of its tough armor.

Although the armadillo belongs to the group called toothless mammals, it does have some small back molars, but these are of little use.

Included in the family of toothless mammals is the group called anteaters, of which the great anteater, or ant bear, is the largest. The little anteater, or tamandua, is the smallest. The pangolin, echidna and aardvark are also popularly known as anteaters, although no actual relationship has been established between the aardvark and this group.

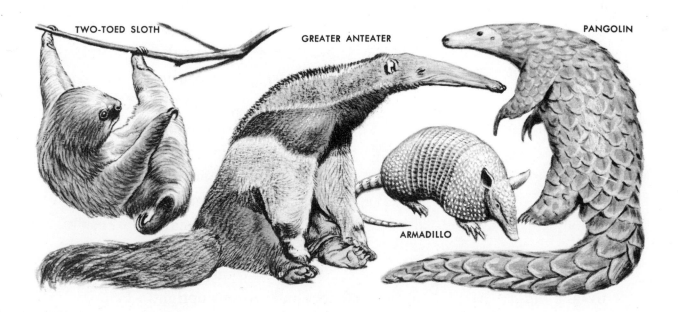

TWO-TOED SLOTH

GREATER ANTEATER

PANGOLIN

ARMADILLO

At the right, a male lion is shown with the lioness and their cubs in the African plains. The leopard, below, is smaller than a tiger or lion. It is the most feared of all cats and lives in Africa and Asia.

WHAT ANIMAL HAS A CLAW IN ITS TAIL?

Most lions live on the treeless or lightly forested plains of Africa, south of the Sahara Desert. The only other lions in the world are the few remaining Indian lions that live in the Gir Forest of northeastern India. These lions are rigidly protected from hunters by the Indian government.

The average lion is a little smaller than a tiger. A male lion may look larger than a tiger of the same size because the lion has a heavy mane covering its neck and shoulders. Not all male lions have manes, however, and no lioness ever does. The manes of wild lions are usually sparse and ragged, due largely to being torn by thorns and bushes and by skirmishes with other lions. But in zoos in northern countries, a lion's mane is likely to grow thick and full. The fur of all lions is short and coarse and is a brownish yellow in color. The mane is usually darker than the rest of the fur. At the tip of a lion's tail is a tuft of dark fur. Within the tuft is a short shaft of horny, naked skin. This is the so-called "claw" or "spur" in a lion's tail. It is not known if this "claw" is useful.

Lions live together in large groups called *prides*. A pride may consist of more than twenty lions of all ages.

WHY IS THE LION CALLED THE KING OF BEASTS?

In ancient times, people regarded the lion as the strongest of all animals. It seemed to fear no enemies and was a stately and dignified-looking animal. These were considered to be kingly qualities, so the lion was said to be the King of Beasts. The lion has long stood for strength and bravery. Warriors who were strong were called lions.

WHAT DO LION CUBS LOOK LIKE?

There are usually four lion cubs in a litter. They are about the size of a house cat, and their eyes are closed until they are six days old. They are striped and spotted, but these markings fade as the cubs grow older. The lioness nurses her cubs until they are three months old, when they begin to eat meat. But they are unable to hunt their own prey until they are about a year old. During this year, the father lion brings food to the nursing lioness, and afterward supplies food to the entire family.

WHO ARE THE HOOFED MAMMALS?

Hoofs are horny casings that cover the toes of some mammals, such as horses, zebras, giraffes, deer, caribou, moose and rhinoceroses. Hoofs protect the toes of animals that usually live in open country and do much running.

Scientists divide hoofed mammals into two main groups: those that have an odd number of toes on each foot, such as the horse and zebra (one toe) and the rhinoceros and tapir (three toes); and those hoofed mammals that have an even number of toes, such as deer, giraffes, bison, camels, goats, llamas and hippopotamuses. Most hoofed animals are even-toed.

WHAT IS THE TALLEST ANIMAL?

The average giraffe is more than fifteen feet tall, and some may be as tall as eighteen feet, which is the equivalent of a two-story-high building. This makes the giraffe, by far, the tallest animal in the world. Almost half its height is due to the animal's long neck. Actually, the giraffe's neck contains only seven neck bones, or vertebrae—the same as the human neck—but each vertebra is very long.

Giraffes live in Africa, south of the Sahara Desert, and feed on the

leaves of acacia and mimosa trees. They pull the leaves into their mouths with long tongues and lips that can be extended far in front of their mouths. The skin of a giraffe is a light sandy color and is covered with dark brown splotches. Thus, in the splotchy shadows of the leaves of a tree, the giraffe gets a natural protective cover from its enemies.

A giraffe has short horns that are about four or five inches long. They are covered with skin and hair and are of little use. When giraffes fight among themselves, they swing their long necks sideways and batter each other with their heads. Against their natural enemies, giraffes kick very powerfully with their long, slender legs. A solid kick from a giraffe can disable a lion. A giraffe can outrun most of its enemies, although a hunter on a fast horse can keep up with the fleeing animal.

For a long time, naturalists believed that a giraffe could not make any sound. Now they know that it can make a low, grunting sound in its throat.

ETRUSCAN SHREW

WHAT IS THE SMALLEST MAMMAL?

Shrews are the smallest mammals, and the smallest shrew is the Etruscan shrew of Mediterranean Europe. This little animal's body measures only one-and-a-half inches in length, and its tail is one-and-an-eighth inches long. It weighs as little as half a teaspoonful of water. The most common shrew in North America is the cinereous or masked shrew, which weighs only as much as a teaspoonful of water. It spends its life under leaves and in runways which it digs under the soil. Its newborn young are smaller than honeybees. To supply its high-strung body, it must eat continually. It eats insects, grubs, earthworms and, sometimes, other shrews.

WHAT IS THE FASTEST ANIMAL?

Although the cheetah is a true member of the feline group, it resembles a dog more than a cat. It has long, slender legs and large, narrow feet. Unlike other cats, but like dogs, the cheetah cannot pull its claws into sheaths in its paws. Its body is slender, but well-muscled. The cheetah's long tail helps it to turn when running fast. Its coat is tawny with black spots. Cheetahs are almost extinct in Asia where they were once plentiful. They now abound mostly in the plains of Africa.

A cheetah can run farther and faster than any other feline, and for a short distance, faster than any other animal. For four or five hundred yards, a cheetah can put on a dazzling burst of speed that may reach seventy miles an hour!

The cheetah, a cat found in Africa and Asia, is the fastest-running land animal in the world.

59

INDEX

Numbers in italics refer to illustrations